Money Matters: Making the Most of

Your Income

Margaret Roane

Money Matters: Making the Most of Your Income

Copyright © 2014 by Margaret Roane, all rights reserved.

To our Heavenly Father, who has lovingly provided for our family through the years, and richly blessed us through His word with the wisdom to make good choices with our finances. We love you!!!

Money Matters: Making the Most of Your Income

Table of Contents

Money Matters: Making the Most of Your Income

Introduction and Scriptural Basis

Why, you may ask, should folks listen to what you have to say about money? Well, my husband Vince and I, parents of three grown sons, have been budget coaches in our church's financial ministry for several years. As budget coaches, we have witnessed many financial situations that could have been avoided if our clients had followed the sound monetary advice found in the Bible.

And what, you may ask, does the Bible have to say about how to manage my money? It will surprise you to learn how much the Bible references your financial life. Here are a few of my favorite verses on the subject of money:

Money Matters: Making the Most of Your Income

The love of money is the root of all evil – 1 Timothy 6:10

Money is certainly an important aspect of life, but you should not be in love with it. Those who pursue financial gain without regard to what is legal and moral will experience problems in life; the same is true for those who prioritize money and possessions above people and relationships. Don't spend so much time working that your relationships or health deteriorate; work/life balance is a great thing!

The rich ruleth over the poor, and the borrower is servant to the lender – Proverbs 22:7

Being overwhelmed with debt puts a damper on your days, and can really restrict your options in life. Resolve now to be strategic with your borrowing so that you keep a manageable to nonexistent debt level. Not all debt is bad, but too much of it or the wrong kind of debt keeps you under pressure and is a real downer! Sometimes you may just need to do without for a while until you can afford what you want.

Render therefore unto Caesar the things which are Caesar's –

Matthew 22:21

Got taxes? You need to pay them. Popular opinion to the contrary, taxes are not a bad thing – they pay for our roads, schools, defense, and other necessary functions of our government. Certainly you can do what you can to legally minimize them, but be honest and don't think they go away if you don't pay them.

...As good stewards of the manifold grace of God – 1 Peter 4:10

A steward is a manager of sorts. God expects us to manage our resources, including our money. For many people, "budget" is a bad word; they prefer to freely spend and charge, hoping their finances will magically balance. Sadly, that is a recipe for disaster! When it comes to your money, you need a plan in place to be sure you arrive at your desired financial destination. A budget is simply an easy-to-make tool that provides a road map for how you will spend your money.

Then he that had received the five talents went and traded with the same, and made them other five talents. And the likewise he that had received two, he also gained other two. But he that had received one went and digged in the earth, and hid his lord's money – Matthew 25:16-18

Don't put your money in a hole in the ground, or under the mattress! You have worked hard for your money, so now your money should be working hard for you. Sometimes we are overwhelmed by the various investment options, and our fear of making a mistake immobilizes us. This book can help you begin to identify great ways to have your money make money.

He that loveth pleasure shall be a poor man; he that loveth wine and oil shall not be rich – Proverbs 21:17

Money Matters: Making the Most of Your Income

We all have should have experiences in life that we enjoy – dinner out, new clothes, vacations, concerts, and more; however, if we spend more than we can afford on the pleasures of life, we will move towards poverty and debt instead of sufficiency and wealth.

For the drunkard and the glutton shall come to poverty: and drowsiness shall clothe a man with rags – Proverbs 23:21

Overindulging in food and alcohol will blow holes in your budget, so moderation is good for your health and your pocketbook. Somehow that early-morning sleep seems sweeter, but if you sleep in instead of going to working, you risk losing your job or business and not having enough income to clothe yourself, so release that pillow and go ahead and face the day. It is said that everything gets better with practice except getting up in the morning – how true!

But thou shalt remember the Lord thy God: for it is he that giveth thee power to get wealth – Deut. 8:18

Money Matters: Making the Most of Your Income

Our ability to work and earn money is a God-given blessing; don't waste that time and energy – take advantage of them and seize the day!

Wherefore do ye spend money for that which is not bread? Isaiah 55:2

It is critical that we differentiate between needs and wants. Needs must be paid for, but wants can be deferred or ignored, based on our available capital.

Take heed, and beware of covetousness: for a man's life consisteth not in the abundance of the things which he possesseth - Luke 12:15

Our culture places a great deal on emphasis on what we have – how large and updated are homes are, whether we have the latest gadgets, what car we drive, if we are wearing the latest fashions with designer labels, what jewelry we own. We have to be careful not to be jealous of celebrities, lottery winners, and others with lots of resources; life is more than what we own. The more we own, the more things we have to maintain. It has been said the best things in life, like salvation, a sunny day, and a beautiful sunset, are free!

Bring ye all the tithes into the storehouse, that there may be meat in mine house, and prove me now herewith, saith the LORD of hosts, if I will not open you the windows of heaven, and pour you out a blessing, that there shall not be room enough to receive it. – Malachi 3:10

As Christians we are responsible for giving our tithe to our places of worship. When we do so, God richly blesses us and provides for our needs. Try it and you will be amazed at what God will do!

He which soweth sparingly shall reap also sparingly; he which soweth bountifully shall also reap bountifully - 2 Corinthians 9:6

In investing and in giving, sowing is required before you can reap, so give and invest generously to reap bountifully in your future.

Money Matters: Making the Most of Your Income

As you can see, the Bible offers a wealth of wisdom on the topic of money. Now let's examine how these lessons apply to us during the financial stages of our lives.

The Roaring Twenties – Entering the Work World

During your teens you sometimes get your first job and your first car, but you really come into your own in your twenties. For some, this stage begins right after high school; for others, it can be after college, graduate school, or the military, but at some point you take over the financial reins of your life. You can make choices now that you will be pleased with in the future.

Your Budget

The first and most important choice is to make a budget and stick to it! A budget is just a plan for where you want your money to go. If you don't have a plan for your money, you will blink and it will just

Money Matters: Making the Most of Your Income

disappear! What should a budget include? It varies according to your situation, but common items are:

- Tithe

- Rent or mortgage

- Food

- Car payment

- Car insurance

- Gas

- Health insurance

- Electricity

- Phone

- Cable

- Water/sewer

- Clothing

- Entertainment

- Car/home maintenance

- Barber/beauty salon

- Medical expenses

- Property taxes if you own a home

- Debt repayment

- Savings

A sample budget is shown in Appendix A. Review your most recent financial records, like your checking account statement or register, to make a list of one month's expenses. Compare your monthly expenses to your monthly income; if you have more expenses than income, you need to reduce expenses, make more money, or both, so that you can cover your expenses. For example, your clothing and entertainment expenditures may need to decrease until you have repaid your debts, or you may need a roommate to help cover your rent. Even a part-time job may be necessary to help make ends meet. Review your budget at least yearly to keep your finances in order, and update your budget when there are changes, such as a new car, new home, or a pay raise ☺. There are many apps and online tools, such as Mint.com, that you can use to accomplish this step if you prefer; a simple spreadsheet or just paper and pencil work as well. Congratulations - you have just taken a huge step towards financial stability!!

Your Emergency Fund

Next on the agenda - start an emergency fund and feed it regularly! We all need some ready cash on hand for unexpected expenses (a flat tire ☹) or opportunities (a great concert coming to town ☺), not to mention situations such as losing your job - where you would need money to stay afloat during a job search. Recommendations for emergency cash range from three to six to eight to twelve months of income, so start saving now and work towards at least six months of living expenses on hand for a rainy day. Use your newly created budget to help you calculate a target amount for your emergency fund (monthly expenses times six would equal your goal). It's best to put this money where it is a little difficult to access; otherwise you may find yourself dipping into it all the time and not making progress towards your savings goals. It's also a great idea to save towards other goals such as vacation, a wedding, or a down payment on a house.

Retirement Savings

Speaking of important savings goals, retirement is one we all want to work toward! I know it seems strange to think about starting to save for retirement when you have just recently joined the working world, but starting in your twenties will tremendously increase the money you will have in retirement. You should begin saving for retirement when you get your first job and keep going until you reach that magic milestone. Sometimes people put off this important task, thinking they can just catch up later, but the benefit of <u>compounding interest</u> over time means that *the money you save in your twenties will work hardest of all for you, so don't put it off*!!! Compounding interest means that you earn interest on previously earned interest; it's how your money makes money for you. This is why time is such a huge help in saving for retirement.

If you are fortunate enough to work for a company with a 401(K) or 403(B) plan that matches a portion of your contribution, you have even *more* of an incentive to get started saving for your retirement. Be sure you contribute up to the point of the match, or you will actually be leaving FREE money on the table! If you don't have the full amount available, start where you can and work your way up with each raise until you are contributing the full amount that will be matched. If your company does not have a matching 401(K) or 403(B) program, contribute to a Roth IRA instead. You can save up to $5000 per year in a Roth, and the earnings will be tax-exempt when you retire – a very sweet deal!! Even if you have a matching 401(K) or 403(B) plan, it is wise to contribute to a Roth IRA with any other funds you have available beyond those you use to get the match (that FREE money!). So be sure to get started saving for retirement in your twenties – even if it is only a few dollars per paycheck. You will be glad that you did!

Your Credit History

You may not even think about your credit unless you apply for a loan, but you should consider your credit score and credit history. Having great credit means you pay less for (or are even able to qualify at all for) car loans, student loans, mortgage loans, and credit cards; you credit score also determines the rates you pay for you car insurance and your homeowner's or renter's insurance. How do you get a great credit score? By paying your bills on time and keeping your consumer debt to a minimum! Your credit history, which is represented by a credit score, makes a big difference in your ability to get loans and in the rates you pay for loans and insurance. Also, many employers check the credit scores of job applicants, so your credit score can even impact your employment opportunities! Check your credit reports at no cost at www.annualcreditreport.com; you may also want to pay to see your FICO score (another name for your credit score) if you will be applying for a major purchase like a car or a house.

Late payments and a high debt-to-credit-limit ratio will hurt your credit history and credit score, so decide on a system that works for you to keep those payments rolling in on time. I pay bills each payday, and my husband pays his bills as they arrive – either is fine as long as you are organized and consistent. By the way, your debt-to-credit-limit ratio is an expression of how much debt you have compared to how much credit you have. If you have several credit cards and they all have been charged to the limit, your debt-to-credit-limit ratio is not a favorable one, and companies will not want to extend more credit to you, especially if you have limited assets (money or property). So be judicious in acquiring debt; when possible, keep your overall debt to a minimum by reserving debt for long-term purchases only, such as a mortgage, a car loan, or college tuition.

Credit Cards

As you can see from our discussion of your credit history, it is important to keep a close eye on your credit card use. I think everyone should have one credit card – it's great for online purchases (safer than a debit card in case of fraud) and the occasional unbudgeted expense or emergency; however, more than one credit card can be your downfall!!! Having multiple cards can mean that debt payments are due several times per month; it is also more difficult to keep track of your overall indebtedness. Using only one credit card means just one debt payment each month, and keeps your total debt amount easily accessible, thereby discouraging overuse of credit. Many times people are unaware of how much debt they have; using only one credit card makes your total debt more obvious to you.

Credit cards are *not* for living beyond your means; if you are consistently running out of money between paydays, you need to reevaluate your budget and make adjustments. Perhaps you need a cheaper apartment or to spend less on entertainment or vacations (see "ways to stretch your cash"). Limit indulgences until you pay down your debt – and remember to distinguish between *wants* and *needs*. Credit cards are so easy to overuse – you may need to give yours a break until you pay it down or preferably, off. The best way to manage a credit card is to only charge what you can pay off in full each month. If an emergency forces you to charge more than that, stop using the card until you pay it off. Remember, you should be budgeting for vacations, clothing, entertainment, and car and household maintenance, not putting those things on your credit card! Most emergencies should be covered by using your emergency fund. Also, be wary of accumulating credit card "points" or "miles" if it means having more debt than you can pay off each month. If you continually find yourself overspending with credit cards, try a cash "diet" – lock up the card(s) and just use cash for a while!

Money Matters: Making the Most of Your Income

Insurance

Be sure you have adequate insurance! It is not wise to attempt to skate by without car insurance or health insurance. One accident and/or health crisis can mean many thousands of dollars of debt. The comparatively small bills for car and health insurance are truly worthwhile. As a renter, you should get renters insurance to protect your possessions from theft or disaster; as a homeowner, you will be required by your mortgage company to have homeowner's insurance; even if you have no mortgage and own your home outright, homeowner's insurance is essential to protect your investment. Once you have a spouse or dependents, add life insurance to your collection to handle the maybes in life; your spouse and children depend on your income to survive, so you would need adequate insurance coverage for their protection in the event of your death. I highly recommend term insurance – it provides the greatest coverage for the smallest price.

Your Car

At the risk of offending some, I suggest that in most cases, it is better to buy, not lease, your automobile. If you buy your car, the money you spend each month on your car payment can eventually stay in your pocket or go into your savings once the car is paid for. If you lease your car, you never reach the point of keeping that monthly payment. We have a goal of keeping our cars until they are 15 years old, as long as we don't have major problems with them. We buy cars that are gently used (in the three- to five-year-old range), so we have many years without car payments. How expensive should your car be? A great rule of thumb is to aim for no more than 36 payments (paying your car off in three years or less). If the car of your dreams does not fit your budget with that payment amount, you can't afford it yet! Keep living, working, and saving – that day will come!

One other note about purchasing a car – arrange your financing separately from your car purchase. We check for the best car loan rates, which are normally with our credit unions, and get our financing with them in advance. Once we went to a small dealership to buy a car, only to be told that this dealership did not sell cars for cash! They made all their profits on the financing. Needless to say we found another car dealer! ☺

Your Housing Expenses

Are you renting an apartment? Be sure you can afford the rent – 30% of your budget would be a good target. Consider a roommate if housing costs in your area are prohibitive, and don't go overboard with furnishings – you don't want to be "house poor", or so strapped for cash that all you can do is sit in your new apartment. Look for apartments in various locations in your city or town – rents can vary significantly depending on your location; remember to consider your commute to work (gas or public transit costs) and your personal safety (priceless!) when choosing your apartment location as well as the price. Also, be sure to calculate related costs such as rental insurance and utilities when determining what rent you can afford. Enjoy having your own place!!

Cosigning

You're off to a great financial start, and then a friend or family member asks you to cosign for their loan. DON'T DO IT!! When you cosign for a loan, you are equally liable for the debt. If your friend doesn't make his or her car payments, you will be responsible for payments on a car that your friend will own – crazy but true if your name is on the loan and not the car title. Consider this – banks have much more money than you, and can afford greater losses than you can even imagine, so if they won't take the risk, you shouldn't either! One of my sons cosigned for a friend's cell phone. The friend ran up the bill to $500.00 and did not pay it, so he had to pay the $500.00 for calls he never made on a phone he did not own.

Many people have been financially buried by cosigning – don't you be one of them!

Whew! That was a lot of information! I know it may seem like a lot to think about, but if you start off in your twenties on a great path, the future decades will fall right into place, and you and your money will get along well for years to come.

The Terrific Thirties

Congratulations – you are officially old!! ☺ Not really – you are just hitting your stride! You're not a kid anymore, and you are moving into a new phase. Here we go!

The Wedding

Whoso findeth a wife findeth a good thing – Proverbs 18:22

Some of you hit this milestone in your twenties, but regardless of the timing, weddings are great! It is a blessing to have someone to share your life, and it is a financial blessing to create economies of scale, as in shared expenses. Remember, however, that you want fond memories and not a mountain of debt from this wonderful day. The

31

two of you should save in advance for your wedding; develop a budget for this event based on your anticipated savings and any contributions from your families. You know how to make a budget from the previous chapter – your expenses cannot exceed your savings and family contributions. Your budget categories would include the church, a venue for the reception, food and beverage costs, the wedding gown itself, flowers, photography, the wedding cake, and the honeymoon.

If you are not a professional athlete or a Hollywood starlet, you should not be imitating an event for the rich and famous! In spite of what you see in the media and read in those fabulous bridal magazines, your guests don't have to eat caviar and your dress need not cost a small fortune or even have a famous designer label. The wedding, although a wonderful day, is only one day. It's the marriage that is most important. Plan an event you can afford and enjoy it. As long as you have found the right person to marry, the most important element of the day is already there. Spend wisely and enjoy yourself, and save plenty of room for the honeymoon in that budget ☺.

Marital Finances

There are many opinions about the best way for married couples to handle their finances. If only one person is working, a "one pot" system may meet your needs (one checking and one savings account), but for many couples today with both spouses working, a "two pot" system better fits their needs (a checking and a savings account for each person, with one credit card per person). This system, which my husband and I use, is a natural fit since most couples would have each had separate accounts prior to the marriage; it also gives each spouse some autonomy in handling money. In this system, shared bills are divided based on the percentage of income each spouse has, e.g., the spouse with 60% of the income pays 60% of the bills. A 50-50 split is only used if incomes are equivalent; otherwise, a 50-50 split would be unfair to the spouse with the smaller income. With the "two pot" system, each spouse has some discretionary income to spend as they please, and each spouse is responsible for the use of his/her credit card and other personal bills, like car payments and clothing. Items to be jointly purchased are allocated as agreed upon by the spouses (we take turns paying for meals out and household repairs), and of course we help each other financially as needed.

A third method is the "three pot" method – his, hers, and ours, with the joint pot used for bill payment and funded on a prorated basis by both spouses. The downside of this method is that one spouse must keep track of two sets of accounts; I find that the "two pot" method works best for most; the "three pot" method is more complicated than necessary, and the "one pot" method can leads to arguments concerning discretionary spending when there are two incomes, not to mention overdrafts with two people accessing one checking account. It is important for newlyweds to come to an agreement concerning how they will handle their money!

Money Matters: Making the Most of Your Income

Buying Your First House

First, let me say that you don't have to try to buy a house and have a wedding at the same time!! It's fine to get married and have an apartment as your first home together while you save up for that down payment. In many cases, you will need 10% of the home's value as a down payment unless you qualify for an FHA loan, which only requires a 5% down payment. Feel free to look around at potential homes while you are saving; you'll want to get an idea of what styles and layouts work for you, what areas of your town you would like to consider, and what price range is right for you so that you will know how much you'll need to save. There will also be closing costs and other fees to cover, and no, you cannot use your emergency fund for your down payment!!!

With your sterling credit histories (you did check your spouse's credit report and FICO score before you said "I do", right?), you will qualify for the best mortgage loan rates, I hope. Your mortgage payment ideally should be no more than 35% of your income. I

suggest you two go to your bank and prequalify before your house

search, so that you know exactly how much house you can afford. If

your budget permits, a 15-year mortgage will save you thousands of

dollars in interest payments; if you must go with a 30-year mortgage,

plan to make additional payments on the principal as long as your

mortgage does not have a prepayment penalty. And if you are still

single, a house or condominium is still a great investment in your

future – go for it!

Furnishing Your First House

Furnish your home slowly, as you can actually afford to do so,

without running up your credit card balance or taking out loans from

furniture stores. Empty rooms are OK! Hand-me-downs and

Goodwill finds are also fine if that is what works in your current

budget. When buying furniture, remember that the financing offered

by furniture stores is often not your best bet – check interest rates carefully and read the fine print in their contracts; your credit card (or definitely cash!) may be a better choice for payment. Don't go deep into debt buying a house full of new furniture all at once, or you risk being "house poor" – meaning you can't afford to go anywhere or do anything except sit on your new furniture in your new house – not fun! You have to walk before you can run, so take your time – you have many years to enjoy your new home.

And Baby Makes Three

A good man leaveth an inheritance to his children's children: and the wealth of the sinner is *laid up for the just. Proverbs 13:22*

Congratulations on the expansion in your family! Check out my parenting book, Parenting Matters: Raising Successful Kids, for great information to help you on your parenting journey. Now that you are a parent, there are some financial matters to consider, specifically a will and adequate life insurance to ensure that your little one will be cared for if something happens to either or both of you. Consider term life insurance; it is the most reasonably priced coverage you can buy. You may also want to name a guardian or trustee in your will to care for your child if anything happens to you both.

This is also the time to start saving for those college expenses using a 529 plan, but only if your emergency fund is at the appropriate level and your retirement savings are on track. Remember, your child can borrow for college, but you cannot borrow for retirement, so don't undermine your retirement savings plan!

As your children grow, you may want to give them an age-appropriate allowance and encourage them to begin saving money as well. Good money habits are passed on from generation to generation, so talk with your children about money during their formative years.

To conserve your cash, consider living in an area where the public schools meet your standards rather than paying tuition for private schools; college tuition will be a sufficient hurdle for your finances!

Finally, babies and children are wonderful, but they do grow up, and they definitely are expensive! Consider your income and decide how many children you can truly afford to have. Also, encourage your kids to get good grades and play sports so that they are eligible for college scholarships when that time comes.

Calculating Your Net Worth

As your thirties draw to a close, you may be wondering, how am I doing financially? I recommend that you periodically calculate your net worth to be sure you are accumulating more assets than liabilities. Simply list the value of your assets (your home, your savings, your car(s), your retirement accounts, and your investments) and of your liabilities (your credit card and other loan balances, your car loan balances, and your mortgage balance). Add up your assets and liabilities separately, and subtract the liabilities from the assets. This should be a positive number, and it should be growing as you move forward through the years. Congratulations on the progress you are making!

The Fantastic Forties and Fifties

College Days for Your Kids

As your children have grown, you have continued to save for their college educations in 529 plans. When the time comes to select colleges for your children, you and the kids need to have a frank discussion about what resources are currently available, how much they will be able to borrow (not as much as students could in years past), and consequently, what schools the family will be able to afford; since you are being financially responsible, money must be a consideration in your child's college choice. It is preferable that parents not incur additional debt for their children's education, as they are busily paying off their mortgage and saving for retirement. If possible, college tuition payments should be limited to cash saved for this purpose in 529 plans and to what students themselves can

41

borrow. If this amount is insufficient for the desired school(s), many students attend a community college for the first two years and then transfer to a four-year school for the final two years, saving a great deal of money in the process. Another cost-saving option is to attend college in the student's hometown and live at home, saving the "room and board" cost.

As you calculate your costs, remember to factor in books, fees, and transportation costs in the college budget. If your child has been saving through the years, those savings and additional earnings by the student during the college years can constitute the student's "pocket money" for miscellaneous expenditures and entertainment. Also consider two-year degree programs, trade schools, apprenticeships and the military as post-secondary options. If your child plans to borrow money for college, be aware that federal student loans are better to acquire than private student loans because they have fixed, lower interest rates. Lastly, have your student be judicious with this option – student loan debt is not dischargeable even in bankruptcy, so don't take on too much!

Burning the Mortgage

I know that some financial advisors would disagree, but if you are in a home you plan to occupy for some time, go ahead and work towards paying off the mortgage. This will give you additional income to save for retirement, and it is a glorious feeling of freedom not to have that mortgage payment each month! When you retire your mortgage, remember to set aside money for property taxes and insurance (if those costs were formerly part of your mortgage payment). *Everyone should plan to pay off their mortgages prior to retirement.* Congratulations on reaching this milestone!

Your Investments

When you are young and have many years of income in your future, it's fine to take some investment risk and weight your retirement savings towards stocks. Of course these stock investments should probably be mutual fund or broad ETFs, and not in just a few individual stocks; this concept is called diversification – spreading your risk. Especially do not invest exclusively in the stock of the company that employs you; if there are problems, you can lose both your job and your savings! Feel free to consult a reputable advisor or to study the many options that exist for investments. For example, you can invest in small, medium and large capitalization companies, domestic, international, and emerging markets, sector funds, commodities, and real estate investment trusts. Limit your investments to reputable companies and to investment vehicles you understand.

As you approach retirement age, your investment mix should become more conservative because you have less time in your working life to recover from bear markets like the one we recently experienced in 2008-2009. One rule of thumb is to have (100 minus your age) percent of your investments in stocks, and the remainder in bonds and/or cash equivalents. One other note – if you change jobs, rollover your retirement savings into your new company's retirement plan or into an IRA. Don't cash out these funds and spend them like they are free money – you will need these savings in your retirement years!

Long Term Care Insurance

Your late fifties are the time to consider buying long term care insurance. Nursing homes, assisted living facilities, and in-home care are all expensive options for our final years, costing thousands of dollars per month. Medicare covers a portion of your medical expenses when you are sick, but it will not cover the custodial care many of us will require when we can no longer perform the activities of daily living such as bathing, dressing, feeding and toileting. Consider getting long term care insurance as part of your financial safety net as long as you can afford the premiums both now and in the future.

Money Matters: Making the Most of Your Income

Caring for Aging Parents and Relatives

Many of us will have the responsibility of caring for and making final arrangements for our aging parents and relatives – this age is called the "sandwich" generation for a reason! We have responsibilities towards our children and our parents at the same time. Financially speaking, you may need to obtain a durable, unlimited power of attorney (POA) to help an aging parent or relative who can no longer handle their personal obligations, including rent or mortgage payments, taxes, and other bills.

Choosing a senior living arrangement is also challenging; look for places that will fit your loved one's finances, and be sure to monitor them on a regular basis so that you can make changes in their living arrangements as necessary. Doctors, hospitals, and rehabilitation facilities will advise you on the level of care your loved one will require. Independent living facilities, such as senior apartment complexes, are the least expensive option and may provide some supports such as transportation to doctor appointments; many also offer onsite activities to encourage residents to interact socially, as well as field trips to shopping centers and other destinations. Assisted living facilities often include medication management and mealtime reminders or services, while nursing home or health care facilities provide round-the-clock medical care as well as all the supports previously mentioned. Referral services can be helpful in locating options, in addition to consulting others in your network of friends and co-workers. Be sure to visit your loved one in any facility often to ensure that they are well cared for in your absence.

Another stage of life will eventually involve making funeral arrangements. At this time of grief, be sure to have a calm, reasonable, friend or family member go with you to help make the arrangements so that you will not overspend on caskets, headstones, and other items. Our parents and relatives would not want us spending undue amounts of money at this time; I know that I would want my children and grandchildren to enjoy the benefits of any remaining funds, not the folks in the funeral industry! If you are the executor for your loved one's will, be aware that this responsibility will require quite a bit of time and effort on your part. Get legal counsel if you need it, and keep good records; there is a final tax return that must be filed the year after your loved one's passing.

Empty Nest - Spend and Save

As we enter the "empty nest" phase, many of us enjoy increased spending on eating out, entertainment, and travel as we savor being "double income no kids" again. But we must also use this time to make a final push towards setting aside adequate resources for retirement. So enjoy reaching this milestone, but be sure to save regularly now that you are in the home stretch racing towards the retirement years. When you are 50 or over, you can make catch-up contributions to your 401(k) or 403(b) plans, so take advantage of that option as well.

The Sensational Sixties and Beyond

Your Retirement Budget

By your sixties, you are closing in on that much anticipated finish line – retirement! Before you actually quit that job you are longing to leave, practice living on your retirement income alone for six months or so. Save the money you won't have for an extra savings boost. If you are not quite ready to make it on the lower income, it's better to find out now rather after you have left that job and moved on; if that's the case, go ahead and work a little longer - then try this again in a year or so!

Collecting Social Security

Your Social Security income will be considerably larger if your wait until your full retirement age to begin collecting it. If you plan to retire before your full retirement age (67 for anyone born after 1960), plan to use other income to bridge the gap. If you can wait until age 70 to begin collecting Social Security, your payout will be even greater!

Medicare

Be sure you sign up for Medicare at age 65, even if you will continue to work. For many of us, 65 is the age when retirement can begin simply because that's when we are eligible for Medicare. Health care premiums are a significant expense, and Medicare is a tremendous help! You will still need supplemental insurance, called Medigap insurance, to help with the things Medicare does not cover. Medical insurance is one of the major and most important costs in retirement.

Estate Planning

Hopefully you completed a will and living revocable trust when you became a parent many years back. However, now is the time to review your documents and consult with your attorney, accountant, and/or estate planner to be sure your affairs will be handled according to your wishes and that tax implications have been considered. Consult with your attorney to ensure that your estate will be properly distributed upon your death, and that the proper instruments are in place to minimize difficulties for your beneficiaries and loved ones. A will is a must for us all, and depending on your state and situation, a revocable living trust may be advisable as well. Advanced medical directives and other documents may be appropriate as well at this point in your life. Please don't fail to plan in this area; your loved ones will truly appreciate your efforts during such a difficult time in their lives.

Money Matters: Making the Most of Your Income

Reverse Mortgages

One way to increase your cash flow after age 62 is with a reverse mortgage. This arrangement does allow you to tap your home's equity while still living in and maintaining ownership of your home, but this benefit comes at a price – the fees can be significant. If you pursue this option, it should be for a monthly payout as opposed to a lump-sum payout. There have been horror stories of folks taking the equity out of their home in a lump sum and later undergoing a foreclosure due to the inability to pay their property taxes and insurance. Seek reliable, objective counsel before taking out a reverse mortgage. Another option to tap your home equity would be to downsize to a smaller, less expensive home; this move will also reduce your property taxes, homeowners' insurance payments, and utility costs.

Remarriage and Prenuptial Agreements

If you suffer the loss of your spouse or have a divorce, be sure to protect your financial future and your assets if you decide to remarry. A prenuptial agreement may be indicated to ensure that your children and grandchildren will still inherit your assets upon your death, and that your assets remain yours during your lifetime regardless of future events.

Now that you've seen the financial steps needed for each decade, consider a few ways to expand your cash flow at any age!

Money Matters: Making the Most of Your Income

Ways to S-T-R-E-T-C-H your Cash

Why does it seem that we often get to the end of our money before we get to the month, or even the end of the pay period? ☺ Here are a few tips to help stretch those dollars so that you can attain your financial goals. You may recognize some of them from other sections of this book:

1) Buy, don't lease your car – a paid-for car means more cash flow for you!

2) Furnish your home slowly, as you can afford to do so – you don't want to be "house poor", right?

3) Replace items as necessary – resist the urge to replace things that work just to have the latest & greatest clothing/appliances/vehicles

4) Seek athletic and academic scholarships for your children – college is an expensive undertaking!

5) Limit meals eaten outside the home, especially with a large family – eating at home can save a lot of money

6) Don't charge more on your credit card than you can pay off each month – credit card debt can really sneak up on you

7) Get a 15-year instead of a 30-year mortgage – you pay less interest and it is over sooner!!

8) Make additional principal payments on your mortgage - for the same reasons

9) Pay off your mortgage before you retire – so you can minimize your expenses in retirement

10) When you pay off your car or home, use the money to retire other debt or save it!

11) Live below your means – much less stressful than living above your means!

12) Use cash – the day always comes when debt has to be repaid

13) Consider a "staycation" or day trips (beach, mountains) instead of a traditional vacation when money is tight – you will have fun without blowing your budget

14) Buy term life insurance instead of whole life or other combination products – you can save or invest the difference in price

15) Consider credit unions instead of banks – they often have better interest rates for savings and loans, as well as free checking

16) Attend community college instead of 4-year schools for the first two years of college – often you take the same courses for a lower price

17) Try having your student live at home during the college years – you and your child will save on "room and board" costs

18) Think about "good debt" (for things that last, like an education) vs. "bad debt" (for things that don't, like clothing or dinner out) – and conduct yourself accordingly!

19) Consider smaller indulgences – like a car wash, a manicure, an ice cream cone

20) Plan a wedding that fits your budget– have a buffet instead of paying per plate, or rent a hall and hire a caterer instead of having the reception at a hotel if it helps you stay within your

budget; if your child is getting married, give the couple what you can afford to contribute and let the couple do the rest

21) Watch those warranties – most are unnecessary

22) Possessions are not a measure of your self-worth; you are more than your possessions

23) Consider gas mileage when buying a car – buy at least one household car with good mileage unless capacity is always needed

24) Perform preventive maintenance on your house and car(s) – fix small problems before they become big ones (a stitch in time saves nine ☺)

25) Donate items you no longer use for tax savings – or have a yard sale and save or enjoy the proceeds

26) Look for free family fun activities or date opportunities – like a picnic in the park

27) Use the library – free bestsellers and videos

28) Keep your car as long as reasonable, repair costs considered - our goal is 15 years!

29) Two can live more cheaply than one – get married or get a roommate to share expenses

30) Consider your budget when thinking about family size –

children are expensive!!

31) Understand advertising and limit your exposure to it – if

shopping is your weakness, don't just hang out at the mall!

Next are some critical keys to generational prosperity for you and

your descendants to use.

Money Matters: Making the Most of Your Income

Keys to Generational Prosperity

There are some basic principles to consider that will mean more money for you, for your children, and for generations to come. Think about these ideas and how they would impact your financial picture.

Marriage Before Children

I saw a statistic on Facebook that stated that children whose parents finish school, get a job, and get married have a 98% chance of avoiding poverty. Teenage pregnancy can mean years of financial struggles, so encourage your children to postpone having children until they are financially ready for the challenge, and married!

Two-parent, Two-income Household

Financially speaking, it is much easier to provide for the needs of a family when there are two working adults, married and committed to each other and the family. Simply put, two can live more cheaply than one due to economies of scale – sharing meals, accommodations, utilities, etc. Two incomes will also mean more income in retirement thanks to Social Security and any applicable pensions, not to mention additional savings due to increased family income through the years. If one parent wants to stay home with the children, do the math and be sure the arrangement makes financial sense for the family.

No More Children Than Your Income Permits

Children are wonderful – one of life's greatest joys. But children are also expensive! Therefore, consideration must be given to the household budget before parents decide to expand their families. Before deciding to have another child, sketch out a new budget with new child care costs, diapers, formula, additional college savings, and other related costs, and envision how it would impact your current lifestyle. Would another child mean fewer or no dinners out, or "staycations" instead of vacations? Once the child is here, there is no going back, so be sure your finances can support the addition without unduly impacting your lifestyle, and/or that everyone is willing to make the lifestyle changes that would be required to support another child in the family.

Parental Focus on Education

In today's competitive job market, having a good education greatly increases your odds of becoming financially secure. Parents who focus on seeing that their children acquire a good education improve the financial outcomes for their children and future generations. Also, children who are educationally successful can qualify for college scholarships, which will also improve their and their parents' bottom line.

Addiction Avoidance

Addictions are expensive undertakings. Whether the addiction is to cigarettes, drugs, alcohol, gambling, food, or shopping, any addiction will blow a hole in your budget. If you suffer from an addition of any sort, counseling is available to help you overcome it, and the cost of counseling pales in comparison to the money the addiction will cost you over time. So get the help you need and plug that hole in your budget!

Home Ownership

Owning your own home does not only give you a sense of belonging to a community and the joy of having your own little corner in the world, it is a tax-advantaged way to save for your future, since you build equity in your home while enjoying tax savings. Finally, when your home is fully paid for, you enjoy the privilege of not paying rent or mortgage payments; your accommodation expense is limited to property taxes, insurance, and maintenance. A home of your own is a goal worth attaining!

Automating your Savings

People who find ways to automate their savings plans are much more successful at accumulating retirement nest eggs and emergency funds. Use payroll deduction, preprogrammed transfers, or any other automated means to ensure that the money you budget for savings actually gets there. Often people will plan to save whatever is left after bills are paid and discretionary spending is spent; however, this approach is very seldom successful. As you have heard from many venues, "pay yourself first" using the automated savings tool(s) of your choice.

Get an Early Start to Retirement Savings

Make a generational habit of beginning your retirement nest egg as soon as you begin your career. Remember that money saved in your twenties and thirties has more time to grow in your retirement accounts; that compounding interest really makes a difference in your ability to accumulate wealth. Many young people don't realize the importance of saving for retirement at an early age; be sure your children understand this vital concept.

Pass your Money Savvy on to Your Kids

There are so many ways to help your children learn to properly manage money, like giving them clothing budgets instead of limitless spending, and summer jobs instead of their parents' credit cards. They can acquire the saving habit, putting aside some of their birthday and Christmas money, babysitting and

Money Matters: Making the Most of Your Income

summer job money, instead of just learning the spending habit; they can learn to give to their church, charities, and the community, to do extra chores to earn extra money, and to manage their checking accounts. You can teach your children money lessons that will last a lifetime, and that they can pass on to future generations as well.

Last but not least, here are your ten financial commandments – the main points you need to remember from this book. Enjoy!

Ten Financial Commandments

Need your financial tips in a nutshell? Here they are:

1) Create a budget

Having a plan for your money is the foundation for your financial success. Knowing where your money is going helps you make spending decisions; your budget also allows you to realistically examine your financial situation and make adjustments in your income and expenses where necessary.

2) Pay your bills on time

Your credit score is heavily influenced by your ability to make timely payments on all your obligations: rent, car note, credit card payments, student loan payments. Your credit score determine the interest rates you pay whenever you borrow money and the insurance premiums you pay; it is also referenced by potential employers, so pay those bills on time and keep your credit score high!

3) Start saving early for retirement

The money you save in your twenties and thirties works hard for you over the years to maximize your retirement nest egg. Compounding interest is a wonderful thing!

4) Accumulate an emergency or "rainy day" fund

Having an emergency fund is a must in today's economy; not only will you have money available to tide you over in case of a job loss, but a cash cushion helps you avoid acquiring credit card debts when life's little emergencies happen (flat tire, leaky faucet, etc.)

5) Annually check your credit reports

You can't be too careful about your credit and good name. Use www.annualcreditreport.com to check your credit with the three major reporting bureaus at no charge. Be sure to resolve any issues so that your credit score is not impacted.

6) Consider buying a home

Having a home is a great way to build wealth in the form of home equity, save on your taxes, and eventually eliminate having a monthly housing payment, so it is a powerful financial tool. Plus it's just great to have a place of your own!

7) Have enough insurance (home/life/car)

Insurance to protect your assets is a must. Be sure you have adequate homeowners and car insurance – the ideal would be replacement value for your home, and comprehensive for your car while its value is substantial and/or you are paying a car loan. Life insurance is needed if you have dependents; be sure to buy term insurance to get the most coverage for the least money.

8) Minimize debt, especially credit card debt

Debt is a drag, and credit card debt is especially annoying because often the items or experiences for which the debt was incurred are long gone – dinners out, vacations, etc. Debt is useful for acquiring an education, a home, or a car (within reason), but endeavor to avoid frivolous debt.

9) Periodically calculate your net worth

Your net worth is your financial scorecard. Even if you are paying your bills on time and sticking to your budget, if your assets are not growing and your liabilities are not shrinking, you are spinning your wheels financially instead of making progress. Your savings and home equity should grow over time and your debts should be shrinking, so that your net worth steadily improves during your working years.

10)   Live within your means

If you constantly spend more than you make, you will always have financial struggles, debts, and declining net worth. If you limit your spending so that you make more than you spend, you can save the excess, reduce your debt, and make steady financial progress over time. No matter how much income you have, if you are spending beyond your means, trouble awaits. There truly is no substitute for living within your means!

Congratulations! You now have all the tools you need to successfully handle your money. Wishing you smooth financial sailing in the years to come!

Appendix A – Sample Budget

Tithe/Offering	200
Rent	750
Food	300
Car Insurance	75
Health Insurance	50
Savings	50
Utilities	195
Phone/Cable	110
Allowance	100
Clothing	50
Hair	25
Entertainment	50
Total Expenses	1960
Net Income	2000
Surplus	40

Topical Index

Money Matters: Making the Most of Your Income

About the Author

Margaret Roane is a professional school counselor from Mechanicsville, Virginia. She began her career as a programmer analyst and an auditor before completing her master's degree in Counseling and transitioning to the field of education. She and her husband Vincent are the proud parents of three grown sons, George, Randy, and Joseph, and the even prouder grandparents of Andrew and Sydney.

www.ingramcontent.com/pod-product-compliance
Lightning Source LLC
Chambersburg PA
CBHW071757170526
45167CB00003B/1062